Cornerstones of Freedom

The Story of
JOHN BROWN'S RAID ON HARPERS FERRY

By Zachary Kent

 CHILDRENS PRESS ®

CHICAGO

National Geographic photograph taken in 1859 of the arsenal at Harpers Ferry

Library of Congress Cataloging-in-Publication Data

Kent, Zachary.
   The story of John Brown's raid on Harpers Ferry.

   (Cornerstones of freedom)
   Summary: Describes the causes, events, and aftermath
of the raid led by John Brown on the United States
arsenal at Harpers Ferry.
   1.   Harpers Ferry (W. Va.) — History — John Brown Raid,
1859 — Juvenile literature.   2.   Brown, John, 1800-1859 —
Juvenile literature.   [1.   Harpers Ferry (W. Va) —
History — John Brown Raid, 1859.   2.   Brown, John, 1800-
1859]   I.   Title.   II.   Title: John Brown's raid on
Harpers Ferry.   III.   Series.
E451.K43   1988   973.7'116   87-35714
ISBN 0-516-04734-5

Childrens Press®, Chicago
Copyright ©1988 by Regensteiner Publishing Enterprises, Inc.
All rights reserved. Published simultaneously in Canada.
Printed in the United States of America.
   2 3 4 5 6 7 8 9 10 R 97 96 95 94 93 92 91 90 89 88

Gunshots cracked the cold gray dawn of October 17, 1859 in Harpers Ferry, Virginia. Awakened by the noise, frightened citizens hastily dressed and gathered in the streets. "What is it?" "What has happened?" they nervously asked one another.

Many of these townspeople worked making weapons at the Harpers Ferry federal arsenal. Now they discovered that during the night a band of northern abolitionists and black slaves had captured the river bridges leading into town and had seized the arsenal buildings. Some important townsmen were being held as hostages.

Bravely, a few Harpers Ferry residents crept toward the arsenal fence for a better look. Within the iron gate they spied a grim-looking old man with a long gray beard. Standing tall and thin, he sternly gazed out at them with his piercing gray eyes.

"That is the leader," whispered one citizen, pointing at John Brown.

Upon first capturing the arsenal the fifty-nine-year-old revolutionary had told the surprised watchman, "I want to free all the Negroes in this state. I have possession of the United States Armory now and if the citizens interfere with me, I must only burn the town and have blood."

Word of Brown's wild plan to give weapons to the slaves filled townspeople with panic. Quickly the alarm spread as church bells clanged and horsemen galloped across the countryside. Virginians hurriedly armed themselves with rifles, shotguns, and pistols and rushed to the town. Most believed that only a madman would attempt such a violent uprising. In the arsenal, however, Brown confidently believed hundreds of slaves soon would come to claim their freedom. Fiercely he insisted, "When I strike, the bees will swarm."

For forty years arguments about slavery had raged in the United States. Thousands of European immigrants were willing to work for low wages in the booming factories of the North. Northerners had no use for slavery. In the South, however, plantation owners depended upon slave labor to plant and pick their crops. Day after day black slaves sweated in their masters' fields.

To many the idea of slavery was tragic. In 1852 a gentle New England woman named Harriet Beecher Stowe wrote a novel called *Uncle Tom's Cabin.* It described the hardships of slavery. Thousands of Northerners who read the book were persuaded that slavery was immoral. In Massachusetts a newspaper editor named William Lloyd Garrison claimed that slavery was a sin and should be outlawed. Garrison

Harriet Beecher Stowe

and others who wanted to do away with slavery were called abolitionists. When Southerners angrily defended their right to own slaves, the problem threatened to tear the country in two.

As new lands west of the Mississippi River were settled, the question arose, "Should slavery be allowed there?" In the Kansas Territory violent clashes erupted between those who wanted slavery and those who opposed it. Soon the entire territory came to be known as "Bleeding Kansas." Five brothers named Brown wrote letters to their father from Kansas describing the fierce struggle. Leaving his New York farm behind, old John Brown vowed to join the fight to keep Kansas free from slavery.

Photo of John Brown (left)
as he looked in 1856
and a sketch of his home
near Osawatomie,
Kansas

John Brown was born in Connecticut in 1800. As a young man traveling across the North, he had failed at one business after another. Yet he managed to raise a family of twenty children. Always deeply religious, Brown became a zealous abolitionist. In Ohio he worked on the Underground Railroad. This secret organization helped runaway slaves escape north to freedom in Canada. In Massachusetts he attended abolitionist meetings and pledged his support to help end slavery. Freed slave and lecturer Frederick Douglass remembered seeing Brown for the first time: "He was lean, strong, and sinewy, built for times of trouble, fitted to grapple with the flintiest hardships. . . . His eyes were gray and full of light and fire."

8

Antislavery activists attacking a proslavery camp

Arriving in Kansas in 1855, Brown threw himself into the antislavery guerrilla war with such wild energy that many people believed he was crazy. Raising a company of followers, Brown rampaged across the countryside. At Pottawatomie Creek he and his men murdered five proslavery settlers, hacking them to death with swords. Vengeful slave owners in turn attacked the town of Osawatomie on August 30, 1856. They burned the houses and shot down Brown's son Frederick in the road. In grief and rage Brown swore, "I have only a short time to live—only one death to die, and I will die fighting for this cause. There will be no more peace in this land until slavery is done for."

Furiously Brown continued fighting. Newspapers called him "Old Brown," "Osawatomie Brown," and "the Old Terrifier." Finally, angered by his lawless actions, President James Buchanan offered a reward for his capture.

A wanted man, Brown grew a beard to disguise himself and made his way across the northern states. Some radical abolitionist friends sheltered him, while others gave him money. Forced out of Kansas, he gradually developed a plan to carry his antislavery fight next into Virginia. For over a year he raised funds, secretly bought weapons, and collected loyal followers.

In July 1859 John Brown rented a Maryland farm. Using the name Smith, he persuaded neighbors that he was a harmless cattle buyer. Just five miles away to the south, across the Maryland border, lay the town of Harpers Ferry, Virginia. Nestled on a hilly point of land where the Potomac and Shenandoah rivers joined, Harpers Ferry contained a U.S. government weapons factory. Brown's revolutionary plan called for the seizure of this arsenal. Then, as local blacks flocked to join his army, he expected to raid farther south in open war against slavery.

During the next few weeks Brown's followers quietly came to the Maryland farm. These volunteers included Kansas abolitionists and three of Brown's sons. Dangerfield Newby, one of the five freed blacks who arrived at the farmhouse, hoped to free his family still enslaved in Virginia. In his pocket he carried a letter from his loving wife. "Oh, dear Dangerfield," it read, "come this fall without fail. . .money or no money, I want to see you so much, that is the one bright hope I have before me." Hidden in the farmhouse attic, these men impatiently awaited their leader's orders.

Overview of the town of Harpers Ferry, Virginia

On October 16, 1859 Brown at last declared the time was right to strike. At eight o'clock that night he left three followers behind to guard supplies and set out with his remaining eighteen recruits. While Brown rode in a one-horse wagon, his men marched two-by-two in the chill, damp darkness. Beneath gray woolen shawls each man carried a Sharps rifle and two pistols.

The peaceful lights of Harpers Ferry twinkled across the river as the raiders reached the covered Potomac River bridge. Brown's men quickly captured the bridge watchman, crossed the bridge, and marched into a small public square. To the right stood the train depot and a hotel called the Wager House. A little farther beyond rose the darkened outlines of the U.S. arsenal buildings.

Hurrying to the armory gate, the men broke the lock with a crowbar. Daniel Whelan, the armory watchman, suddenly found himself surrounded. Forced to remain silent, Whelan watched as Brown sent men to capture the second river bridge and Hall's Rifle Works farther away on Shenandoah Street. Brown next selected a brick building containing arsenal fire-fighting equipment as his headquarters. From this engine house, the old man sent raiders into the surrounding countryside to cut telegraph wires and kidnap hostages.

Brown's men held some people hostage in the arsenal (above).
Later, the hostages were moved to the engine house where the final
battle took place.

All remained quiet in Harpers Ferry until shortly
after midnight. A second railroad watchman walked
to the Potomac bridge and discovered Brown's
guards there. As he ran away they fired at him,
grazing his scalp with a bullet. Not long afterwards
the train from Wheeling chugged into town. When
the conductor learned of the danger on the bridge
ahead, he stopped the train.

Carefully the conductor, along with a few passengers and railroad workers, crept toward the bridge to investigate. "Halt!" cried out a voice from the bridge. Frightened, the men turned and fled. Shots rang out and the station baggage clerk, Shephard Hayward, staggered with a deadly wound. "I am shot!" he moaned as his friends dragged him away. In a strange twist of fate, Hayward, himself a freed slave, became the first victim of John Brown's plan to free the slaves.

Through the murky morning hours raiders returned to the armory with the hostages they had rounded up, their household weapons, and a few of their slaves. The most important of these captives was Colonel Lewis W. Washington, a wealthy local planter and a great-grandnephew of George Washington. John Brown strapped around his waist a beautiful sword that Washington owned. The family heirloom had been given to the first president by King Frederick the Great.

As arsenal employees arrived at the gate for work, they also became hostages. Before long, Brown's men guarded over forty prisoners. Staring at them by flickering torchlight, Brown told his prisoners the terms for their ransom. He would free each man in exchange for a "stout Negro."

Original drawing made by a reporter who was covering the battle between militia volunteers in the armory yard and Brown's raiders in the engine house.

All the unexpected noise and gunshots scared Harpers Ferry citizens. Some hurriedly packed belongings and escaped from town. Others huddled on street corners and wondered what was going on. One man jumped upon his horse and rushed to the nearby county seat of Charlestown to warn the people there. Another fearless man, grocer Thomas Boerly, fired into the armory yard from across the street, until one of the raiders shot him dead.

COLONEL LEWIS WASHINGTON

Four miles from the ferry, raiders entered the home of Col. Lewis Washington (a gentleman farmer and slaveowner), capturing him and twelve of his slaves.

DANGERFIELD NEWBY

Though born a slave, Dangerfield Newby's father (a Scotchman) took the family to Ohio where they were freed. Later Dangerfield married a slave woman who was the property of a man in Virginia. After Dangerfield's death at Harpers Ferry, his wife and six children were "sold south."

Near dawn Brown foolishly granted the safe passage of the train. Once across the Potomac bridge, the train roared on to Monocacy Station where the telegraph lines remained intact. Soon the wires hummed, carrying the train conductor's panicked message north and south:

"AN INSURRECTION HAS BROKEN OUT AT HARPERS FERRY, WHERE AN ARMED BAND OF ABOLITIONISTS HAVE FULL POSSESSION OF THE GOVERNMENT ARSENAL AND THE TOWN. . . . THE INSURRECTIONISTS SAY THEY HAVE COME TO FREE THE SLAVES AND INTEND TO DO IT AT ALL HAZARDS."

The thought of a widespread slave uprising alarmed Marylanders and Virginians. Fearing their homes could be looted and their families murdered at any moment, farmers and villagers grabbed their guns and marched to Harpers Ferry. By noon of October 17, hundreds of these volunteers were pouring into the town. Blistering gunfire soon drove Brown's guards from the river bridges and from Hall's Rifle Works. "Let go on them!" yelled Old Brown to his raiders in the armory yard. Rifles cracked across the square. Wounded volunteers crawled away, while their comrades scurried for cover. Among the raiders, Dangerfield Newby suddenly clutched his neck and fell. The first of John Brown's men to die, Newby would never see his enslaved wife and children again.

Brown had expected friendly slaves to rush to Harpers Ferry, not angry militiamen. Stunned by the swiftness of this attack, he now realized he was trapped. With ten of the most important hostages, Brown and his remaining raiders retreated into the safest part of the engine house and swung its big doors closed.

Hoping to negotiate a cease-fire that would allow his men to escape, Brown sent raider Will Thompson out waving a white handkerchief. The wildly excited crowd seized Thompson at the first opportunity and tied him up. A little later Brown tried again. Aaron Stevens and Brown's son Watson reached the square when the mob opened fire. Stevens fell thrashing with six bullets in his body. Although a bullet tore into his chest, Watson Brown crawled back to his father in the engine house.

All through the afternoon bullets whistled and gunsmoke clouded the Harpers Ferry streets. When raider Will Leeman tried to escape by swimming across the river, militiamen shot him down. The kindly old mayor of Harpers Ferry, Fontaine Beckham, peered out from behind the railroad water tower to get a better look at the engine house. A single shot, and Mayor Beckham crumpled to the ground dead.

Interior of the engine house

In revenge, townspeople furiously dragged their prisoner Will Thompson to the railroad bridge. At close range they fired pistols into Thompson's body and dumped him over the side. Barely alive, Thompson struggled through the bloodied water until he reached a little rocky island. From the bridge drunken militiamen afterwards used his body for gruesome target practice.

Colonel Robert E. Lee

As darkness fell Brown ordered his few uninjured raiders to chip loopholes in the brick walls through which they could fire their guns. During the afternoon a bullet struck young Oliver Brown. Now he lay on the floor groaning in agony and pleading to be killed. Grimly his father told him, "If you must die, die like a man." Later the old man called out to Oliver, but got no answer. "I guess he is dead," he quietly commented.

Outside the arsenal, Harpers Ferry buzzed with activity. Militiamen crowded the hotel barrooms, the streets, and bridges, drinking and laughing, thrilled by the day's gory adventure. Witness Edward White recalled, "About midnight we heard the whistle of an engine and hastened to the station. Very soon a long train from Baltimore came steaming in. It brought a body of U.S. marines (some ninety in number) commanded by Col. Rob't E. Lee (afterwards the great Confederate general). With him were Lieut. J. E. B. Stuart (afterwards the Confederate cavalry leader), who had volunteered for the occasion, and Lieut. Israel Green of the Marine Corps. . . ." With orders from President Buchanan, Colonel Robert E. Lee took control of the situation and planned an attack on the engine house.

At daybreak on October 18, hundreds of curious militiamen and spectators crammed the street outside the arsenal. They crowded the windows of the surrounding buildings and filled the raised railroad platform that overlooked the engine house. Before them two squads of marines fixed bayonets on their muskets, hefted sledgehammers, and prepared their assault.

U.S. marines breaking down the door of the engine house

Inside the engine house, John Brown waited. The hostage, Colonel Washington, observed that Brown "was the coolest and firmest man I ever saw in defying danger and death. With one son dead by his side, and another shot through, he felt the pulse of his dying son with one hand and held his rifle with the other, and commanded his men. . .to sell their lives as dearly as they could."

After a few moments Lieutenant Stuart approached the engine house door. Brown opened it a crack but refused Stuart's demand that he surrender. In an instant Stuart jumped aside and waved his hat to signal the waiting marines. With a shout the men charged the little brick building. Cheers roared from the watching crowd, as marines attacked the thick doors with sledgehammers. When the wood refused to budge, the marines next picked up a heavy ladder to use as a battering ram. "Once—twice—the impromptu battering ram thundered upon the door," recalled Edward White. "Suddenly there was a tremendous crash and a fragment of the door. . .extending from top to bottom, was hurled in upon the defenders."

Inside the engine house the raiders fired desperately through loopholes and cracks. Noise, confusion, and gunsmoke filled the yard as Lieutenant Green dashed through the broken doorway followed by his men. One marine pinned a screaming raider to the wall with his bayonet. Another stabbed a raider as he crawled under the fire engine.

"This is Osawatomie," called out the hostage Colonel Washington, pointing at John Brown. The bearded old abolitionist knelt by the door reloading his rifle. Lieutenant Green leaped upon him and brought his sword down on Brown's head. A second blow struck Brown's belt or buckle, bending the marine officer's sword in half. Swinging his sword like a club, Green at last beat the old man to the floor unconscious.

John Brown's capture

John Brown's raid on Harpers Ferry had lasted just thirty-six hours and had cost seventeen lives. Of the raiders, ten lay dead or dying and five had been captured. The others escaped into the mountains.

Marines carried Brown out of the engine house, his hair and beard covered with blood. Completely defeated, the old man lay in the grass as newspapermen pressed in close. "What was your. . .object?" asked one reporter. "To free the slaves from bondage," calmly answered Brown. The excited Harpers Ferry mob wanted the old man hanged at once. When Virginia governor Henry A. Wise arrived that afternoon, however, he promised that Brown would receive a fair trial.

John Brown after his capture

John Brown lay on a cot during his trial for murder, treason, and rebellion.

That night marines took the surviving raiders by train to the county jail in Charlestown. On October 26 John Brown's seven-day trial began. Every day hundreds of people packed the Charlestown courtroom to watch the case. In truth, the entire nation had focused its attention on John Brown and his stunning raid. Southerners claimed Brown was a crazed abolitionist intent on starting civil war. The Richmond *Inquirer* announced: "The Harpers Ferry invasion has advanced the cause of Disunion more than any other event that has happened since the formation of the Government." Many Northerners, however, sympathized with Brown's desire to free the slaves. "John Brown may be a lunatic," claimed one Boston paper, but if so "one-fourth of the people of Massachusetts are madmen."

During the trial Brown lay on a cot nursing his wounds and listening to the evidence against him. Brown's hostages admitted that the old man had treated them with courtesy. The lawless uprising and shocking bloodshed at Harpers Ferry, though, clearly sealed his fate. On November 1 the jury found John Brown guilty of murder, treason, and rebellion, and the next day the judge sentenced him to hang. Rising from his cot Brown addressed the hushed courtroom with deep religious feeling.

"I deny everything but what I have all along admitted: the design on my part to free slaves. . . . I believe that to have interfered as I have done. . .was not wrong but right. Now if it is deemed necessary that I should. . .mingle my blood with the blood of my children and with the blood of millions in this slave country. . .I submit. So let it be done."

From his jail cell during the following days Brown wrote scores of letters and granted newspaper interviews. Aroused Northerners considered Brown a martyr, and the old man quickly saw a chance to strike a blow at slavery. When he learned that some abolitionists wished to break him out of jail, he rejected the idea. "Let them hang me," he exclaimed, "I am worth inconceivably more to hang than for any other purpose."

On the clear, warm morning of December 2, 1859, John Brown's jailers led him out into the sunshine. To one guard the fiery old man handed a last scribbled warning to his countrymen: "I, John Brown am now quite *certain* that the crimes of this guilty land will never be purged *away;* but with Blood."

Wearing his old suit, a new black slouch hat, and a pair of red slippers, Brown climbed onto a waiting wagon. He sat on his own coffin, as two white horses drew the wagon past rows of militia guards. The wagon rattled past the Blue Ridge Mountains toward a field outside Charlestown, and Brown quietly remarked, "This is a beautiful country. I never had the pleasure of seeing it before." When

the wagon reached the wooden gallows, Brown mounted the steps and removed his hat. His jailer placed the noose around his neck and covered his head with a heavy cloth hood.

Fifteen hundred militiamen filled the field and stood at attention. Among these witnesses was a professor of the Virginia Military Institute. During the American Civil War people would remember him as Confederate general Thomas "Stonewall" Jackson. Standing with another militia company was a stage actor from Maryland named John Wilkes Booth. Booth would shock the nation in 1865 by murdering President Abraham Lincoln at Ford's Theatre. Unaware that they would soon take their own places in history, these men watched as John Brown met his death.

The sheriff ordered Brown to step forward to the platform trap. "I can't see, gentlemen," the old man answered. "You must lead me." His guards walked him to the spot. With quiet dignity he waited, until at last the sheriff took an ax and chopped the rope holding up the trap. Heavily John Brown dropped and dangled from his noose. A light breeze blew the lifeless body to and fro as militia colonel J.T.L. Preston called out, "So perish all such enemies of Virginia! All such enemies of the Union! All foes of the human race!"

Friends transported John Brown's corpse to North Elba, New York, where it was buried on the family farm. His body lay at rest, but memories of his Harpers Ferry raid would not. In death John Brown became a legend, and more than ever Northern abolitionists demanded that slavery be ended.

The violent debate reached its climax in 1860 when Abraham Lincoln of Illinois was elected presi-

dent of the United States. Angry Southern slaveholders feared that Lincoln intended to abolish slavery. Rather than submit, eleven slave states quit the Union and formed the Confederate States of America.

In April 1861 the Civil War began when Confederate cannon bombarded Fort Sumter, a Union fort in the harbor of Charleston, South Carolina. As John Brown predicted, four long years of bloody fighting lay ahead. The cost to win the slaves their freedom and finally reunite the nation would be 600,000 American lives.

During the war the western portion of Virginia, including Harpers Ferry, remained loyal to the United States. In 1863 it became the new state of West Virginia. Strategically located, Harpers Ferry saw Northern and Southern troops fight back and forth through the town an astonishing twenty-three times. Confederate soldiers tramping along the cobbled streets sometimes cursed the fierce old man they claimed had sparked the war. Union troops, however, striding toward victory often loudly sang the song that came to symbolize their cause:

> "John Brown's body lies a-mouldering in the grave,
> John Brown's body lies a-mouldering in the grave,
> John Brown's body lies a-mouldering in the grave,
> But his soul is marching on."

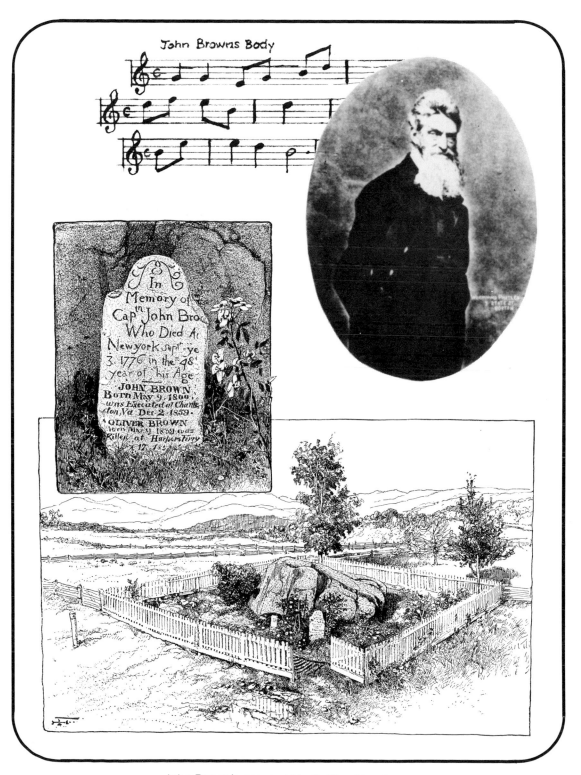

John Brown's grave at North Elba, New York

Current photo of Harpers Ferry taken from Maryland Heights

PHOTO CREDITS

Harpers Ferry National Historical Park—4, 15, 16 (2 photos), 19, 21,
   27, 29, 31 (top right)
Historical Pictures Service, Chicago—1, 2, 7 (2 photos), 9, 11,
   13, 20, 23, 24, 25, 31
Kansas State Historical Society—8
Roloc Pictorial Research—32
Charles Hills—Cover

About the Author

Zachary Kent grew up in Little Falls, New Jersey, and received an English degree from St. Lawrence University. Following college he worked at a New York City literary agency for two years and then launched his writing career. To support himself while writing, he has worked as a taxi driver, a shipping clerk, and a house painter. Mr. Kent has had a lifelong interest in American history. Studying the U.S. presidents was his childhood hobby. His collection of presidential items includes books, pictures, and games, as well as several autographed letters.